WIDE EYED EDITIONS

THE HELLO ATLAS

EUROPE

ASIA

OCEANIA

AFRICA

HOW TO USE THIS BOOK

The Hello Atlas has been designed to give you a taste for the rich diversity of languages spoken across the world today. Before you start, ask for the help of an adult to download the app that accompanies this book. The app is free to download and is available on the App Store® and on Google Play™.

Sorted by continent, this book features a variety of languages, some of which you'll recognize—and some that might be new to you!

To start, turn to the continent map at the beginning of each chapter to learn about the main language groups, or language families that are spoken there.

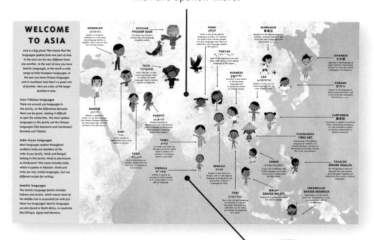

On this map you'll discover which languages feature in this chapter, with each one's English name, the name as it's written in the language, and a short description about every one.

SINHALA
සිංහල
Sinhala is spoken by around 20 million people in Sri Lanka where it is an official language.

AVIRO

HALO!

BONJOUR

Follow along with your app, which is structured like the book, so that you can hear the phrase spoken while looking at the pictures.

We have searched the world over for native speakers of every language featured in this book, and have recorded more than 130. However, a handful have so far proved too remote to capture, and we'd love to hear from anyone who would like to contribute to this project at the address listed on the back page.

NI HAO!

HEI!

WAQUAA!

On the pages that follow you'll find pictures of children in everyday scenes, greeting you in different ways: saying hello, telling you their name, and wishing you a happy birthday!

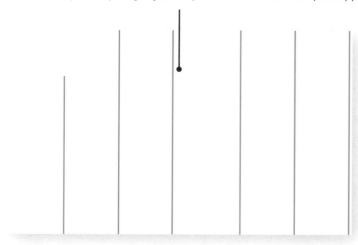

In each of these pictures, you'll discover the English phrase and the translation, written with the Roman alphabet. We have Romanized languages that don't use Roman script (like Korean for example) and simplified the writing so that every phrase in the book can be spoken . . . by you!

Finally, flip to the "Further Phrases" section at the back of the book to discover more for every language, all of which can be heard on your app.

So—pick your destination and begin your language adventure . . . who will you say hello to today?

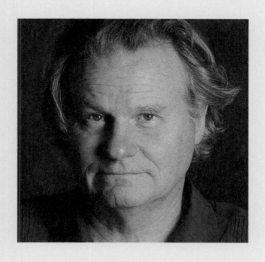

FOREWORD
by Professor Wade Davis

I cannot imagine a world in which I could not speak English, for not only is it a beautiful language, but it is my language, the full expression of who I am.

Around the world, 7,000 languages are spoken, but of this huge variety, 80 percent of the world's population communicates with one of just 83 languages. This means that some 3,500 languages are kept alive by a tiny 0.2 percent of the global population, and more than 600 of them have fewer than a hundred speakers left. By contrast, the ten most prevalent languages are thriving; they are the mother tongues of half of humanity.

But what of the poetry, songs, and knowledge woven into those languages spoken by small groups of people, who together represent 98.8 percent of the world's linguistic diversity? Is the wisdom of an elder any less important simply because they cannot be understood by the majority of the world? Would it be easier for us to understand one another if we left the lesser-spoken languages to be forgotten?

We think quite the opposite—for each language encapsulates a culture, and forms a vital branch of humankind's family tree, a store of our knowledge and experience. Whatever corner of the world you're reading from, The Hello Atlas is an invitation to explore the great diversity of language, and experience the gift that it gives: hope, inspiration, and a promise for the future.

Wade Davis is Professor of Anthropology and the BC Leadership Chair in Cultures and Ecosystems at Risk at the University of British Columbia. Between 1999 and 2013 he served as Explorer-in-Residence at the National Geographic Society. Author of 19 books, including *One River*, *The Wayfinders* and *Into the Silence*, winner of the 2012 Samuel Johnson prize, he holds degrees in anthropology and biology, and received his Ph.D. in ethnobotany, all from Harvard University.

WELCOME TO EUROPE

Europe represents, geographically, one half of the large language family known as Indo-European. The majority of languages spoken in Europe are a part of this family. European languages broadly belong to three families and are some of the most widely spoken in the world.

Romance languages

A number of languages spoken in Europe evolved directly from Latin, and these are often called Romance languages. You'll see many similarities in some of the words used in these languages in everyday life. See if you can pick some out. Languages in this little family include Catalan, French, Spanish, Portuguese, Italian, and Romanian.

Germanic languages

This group of languages is the largest language family in Europe. German, English, Swedish, Danish, and Dutch are all members. Notice the word for "hello" in these languages and you'll see just how close they are.

Slavic languages

Many of the languages of Eastern Europe are Slavic languages. Russian, Polish, Czech, and Croatian are all members of this family. Slavic languages remain quite close and speakers of one can often understand those of another.

ICELANDIC
ISLENSKA

This Germanic language hasn't changed much in the last thousand years and speakers today can read very old texts.

ENGLISH

English is the most widely spoken language in the world—it's an official language for almost 60 countries!

GAELIC
TEANGACHA GAELACHA

Scotland and Ireland are home to Gaelic—it's an important part of their history and national identities.

WELSH
CYMRAEG

The Celtic language Welsh is closely related to the language of Breton, spoken in the west of France.

BRETON
BREZHONEG

Breton has evolved from people who left Britain in the middle ages and settled in northern France.

FRENCH
FRANÇAIS

French is one of the most-learned languages. It's known as the language of love—a true romance language!

SPANISH
ESPAÑOL

Spanish is one of the most widely spoken languages in the world—heard on almost every continent.

PORTUGUESE
PORTUGUÊS

Portuguese was taken all over the world by explorers of the 15th and 16th centuries.

CATALAN
CATALÀ

Catalan is mostly spoken northeast Spain and southeast France—and you'll certainly hear it spoken in Barcelona!

NORWEGIAN
NORSK
Speakers of Norwegian, Danish, and Swedish can often understand each other because they are closely related.

FINNISH
SUOMEN KIELI
Finnish is spoken in Finland and is thought to be quite a difficult language for English speakers to learn.

RUSSIAN
РУССКИЙ ЯЗЫК
Russian has the most speakers of any language in Europe. It's a Slavic language and is written in Cyrillic script.

SWEDISH
SVENSKA
Swedish is descended from Old Norse—a dead language from which Danish and Norwegian also came.

LATVIAN
LATVIEŠU VALODA
Latvian is in the Baltic language family and is related to its neighbor: Lithuanian.

DANISH
DANSK
Danish is in the Scandinavian language family, which is a part of the Germanic family.

LITHUANIAN
LIETUVIŲ KALBA
This old language may sound a lot like the first language that all Indian and European languages evolved from.

GERMAN
DEUTSCH
German is a Germanic language and one of English's closest relatives.

POLISH
JĘZYK POLSKI
The "pole" in "Polish" means "field" in the language—a reflection of the low flat lands of the country.

DUTCH
NEDERLANDS
Dutch is spoken in the Netherlands and in parts of Belgium where it's sometimes called Flemish.

SLOVAK
SLOVENČINA
Slovak is related to Czech and speakers of the two languages can usually understand each other!

ROMANIAN
LIMBA ROMÂNĂ
Romanian is spoken not only in Romania, but also in Moldova. It's a Romance language.

CZECH
ČEŠTINA
The Czech Republic is home to Czech. It's a Slavic language closely related to Slovak.

HUNGARIAN
MAGYAR
Hungarian counts Finnish as one of its closest relatives—even though they are spoken in two distant countries.

SERBIAN
СРПСКИ
Speakers of Serbian and Croatian can understand each other very easily.

CROATIAN
HRVATSKI
Croatian is a member of the Slavic language family, and is closely related to Serbian.

ITALIAN
ITALIANO
Italian communities can be found all over the world. Today, everyone knows a little Italian, even if it's just "spaghetti!"

GREEK
ΕΛΛΗΝΙΚΆ
Greek is known as a Hellenic language—but it's a very small family—just Greek! It even has its own alphabet.

TURKISH
TÜRKÇE
Turkish is an unusual language in Europe, in that it's more closely related to Asian languages east of the continent.

Mi chiamo Maria.

My name is Maria.

Ciao!

Hello!

This is Maria and Mario. They speak **ITALIAN**.

¡Qué día tan bonito!

What a beautiful day!

This is Santiago. He speaks **SPANISH**.

Bună ziua.

Good day.

Adriana speaks **ROMANIAN**.

Olá.

Hello.

João speaks **PORTUGUESE**.

Var kommer du ifrån?

Where do you come from?

This is Alice. She speaks **SWEDISH**.

Hola!

Hello!

Com està?

How are you?

Bon profit!

Enjoy your meal!

This is Caterina. She speaks **CATALAN**.

Wie heißt du?

What is your name?

Ich heiße Felix.

I'm called Felix.

This is Felix. He speaks **GERMAN**.

Hallo.

Hello.

Fijne Verjaardag!

Happy birthday!

Tot ziens!

See you later!

This is Isa. She speaks **DUTCH**.

It's a beautiful day!

It's a beautiful day!

George speaks **ENGLISH**.

Hej!

Hello!

Rart at møde dig.

Nice to meet you.

Freja speaks **DANISH**.

This is Svein. He speaks **NORWEGIAN**.

This is Bjork. She speaks **ICELANDIC**.

This is Mikko. He speaks **FINNISH**.

Ochen prijatno.

Pleased to meet you.

Anastasia speaks **RUSSIAN**.

Cześć.

Hello.

Mam na imię Artur.

My name is Arthur.

This is Artur.
He speaks **POLISH**.

Zdravo!

Hello!

This is Nada. She speaks **SERBIAN**.

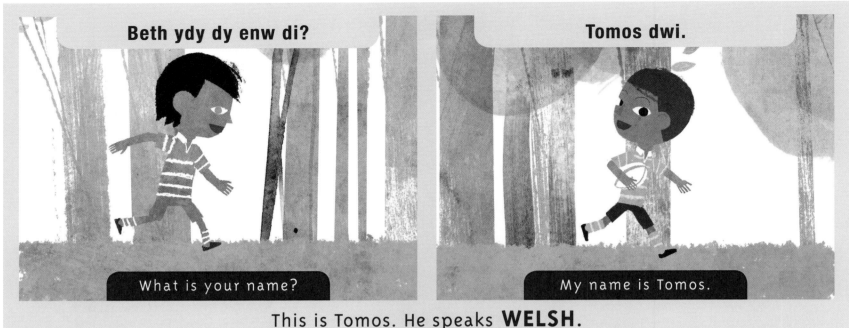

Beth ydy dy enw di?

What is your name?

Tomos dwi.

My name is Tomos.

This is Tomos. He speaks **WELSH**.

Hogy vagy?

How are you?

This is Eszter. She speaks **HUNGARIAN**.

Labdien.

Hello.

Karlis speaks **LATVIAN**.

Malonu susipažinti.

Pleased to meet you.

Elgé speaks **LITHUANIAN**.

This is Josip. He speaks **CROATIAN**.

This is Andrej. He speaks **SLOVAK**.

Dobrý den!

Hi!

Jak se máš?

How are you?

Mám se dobře.

I'm fine.

This is Ivona. She speaks **CZECH**.

Ya su!

Hello!

This is Ajax. He speaks **GREEK**.

Adım Reyyan.

My name is Reyyan.

Sonra görüşürüz.

See you later.

Reyyan speaks **TURKISH**.

WELCOME TO ASIA

Asia is a big place! This means that the languages spoken from one part of Asia to the next can be very different from one another. In the west of Asia you have Semitic languages, in the south a wide range of Indo-European languages, in the east you have Chinese languages, and in Southeast Asia there's a great mix of families. Here are a few of the larger language families in Asia.

Trans-Himalayan languages

There are around 400 languages in this family, so the differences between them can be significant, making it difficult to spot the similarities. The most spoken languages in this family are the Chinese languages (like Mandarin and Cantonese), and Burmese.

Indo-Aryan languages

Most languages spoken throughout northern India are members of the Indo-Aryan family. Hindi and Bengali belong in this family. Hindi is also known as Hindustani—this name includes Urdu, which is spoken in Pakistan. Hindi and Urdu are very similar languages, but e different scripts for writing.

Semitic languages

The Semitic language family includes Hebrew and Arabic, which means most of the Middle East is accounted for with just these two languages! Semitic languages are also found in North Africa, in countries like Ethiopia, Egypt, and Morocco.

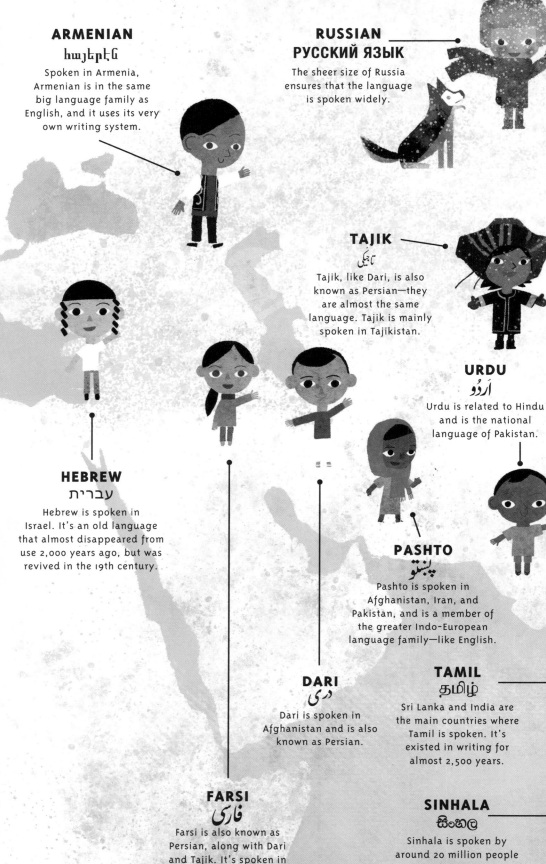

ARMENIAN
հայերէն
Spoken in Armenia, Armenian is in the same big language family as English, and it uses its very own writing system.

RUSSIAN
РУССКИЙ ЯЗЫК
The sheer size of Russia ensures that the language is spoken widely.

TAJIK
تاجیکی
Tajik, like Dari, is also known as Persian—they are almost the same language. Tajik is mainly spoken in Tajikistan.

URDU
اُردُو
Urdu is related to Hindu and is the national language of Pakistan.

HEBREW
עברית
Hebrew is spoken in Israel. It's an old language that almost disappeared from use 2,000 years ago, but was revived in the 19th century.

PASHTO
پښتو
Pashto is spoken in Afghanistan, Iran, and Pakistan, and is a member of the greater Indo-European language family—like English.

DARI
دری
Dari is spoken in Afghanistan and is also known as Persian.

TAMIL
தமிழ்
Sri Lanka and India are the main countries where Tamil is spoken. It's existed in writing for almost 2,500 years.

FARSI
فارسی
Farsi is also known as Persian, along with Dari and Tajik. It's spoken in Iran and Iraq.

SINHALA
සිංහල
Sinhala is spoken by around 20 million people in Sri Lanka where it is an official language.

HINDI
हिन्दी

Hindi is one of the official languages of India. It's claimed by almost half a million people as a first language—but there are more than 700 languages spoken in the country.

MANDARIN
官話

Mandarin is the official language of China; everyone learns it. But China has many languages and most people speak at least two.

JAPANESE
日本語

Japanese is the language of Japan and has a mysterious history—it's not clear which languages it is related to.

NEPALI
नेपाली

High in the Himalayas you find Nepal, and Nepali is the official language of the region.

BURMESE
မြန်မာစကား

Burmese is also known as the Myanmar language and is spoken by almost 50 million people.

LAO
ພາສາລາວ

Spoken in Laos, Lao is a tonal language, like its close relative, Thai.

KOREAN
한국어

Korean is the language of North and South Korea, and is one of the few languages that has no known relatives.

CANTONESE
廣東話

Cantonese is spoken in southern China, Hong Kong, and Macau. It's also commonly spoken in Chinese communities in Western countries.

VIETNAMESE
TIẾNG VIỆT

Vietnamese is the official language of Vietnam. It is related to Khmer, but due to borrowing words from Chinese, this is not very obvious!

KHMER
ភាសាខ្មែរ

If you visit Cambodia, this is the language you'll need. It has a very complicated writing system.

TAGALOG
WIKANG TAGALOG

The Philippines is home to Tagalog—but also another 180 languages! Tagalog and English are the country's official languages.

BENGALI
বাংলা

Bengali is also known as Bangla, and it is the official language of Bangladesh and one of the 22 official languages of India.

INDONESIAN
BAHASA INDONESIA

Indonesian is of course the language of Indonesia. It's an extremely close relative of Malaysian.

THAI
ภาษาไทย

Thai is the national language of Thailand. It's a tonal language—the pitch and inflection of your voice can change the meaning of a word!

MALAY
BAHASA MELAYU

Malaysian is spoken by almost 300 million people.

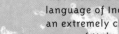

Halo.

Hello.

Senang bertemu dengan Anda.

Pleased to meet you.

Selamat tinggal.

Goodbye.

This is Intan. She speaks **INDONESIAN**.

Nama saya Syukri.

My name is Syukri.

Syukri speaks **MALAY**.

Magandang araw sa'yo!

Have a good day!

Amihan speaks **TAGALOG**.

Johm riab sua.

Hello.

Sok speaks **KHMER**.

Ja ma nau na me Thiri ba.

My name is Thiri.

This is Thiri. She speaks **BURMESE**.

Xin chao.

Hello.

This is Linh. She speaks **VIETNAMESE**.

Neih hou.

Hahng wuih.

Hello.

Pleased to meet you.

This is Tai.
He speaks **CANTONESE**.

Konnichiwa.

Hello.

This is Yukiko. She speaks **JAPANESE**.

Ni hao.

Hello.

Hen gaoxing renshi ni.

你好

Pleased to meet you!

Wo jiao Feng.

My name is Feng.

This is Feng. She speaks **MANDARIN**.

Nae ireumeun Okkyun iyeyo.

My name is Okkyun.

Okkyun speaks **KOREAN**.

Sabaai-dii!

Hello!

This is Konala.
He speaks **LAO**.

Nomoshkar.

Hello.

Apnar din bhalo katu!

Have a nice day!

This is Sujit. He speaks **BENGALI**.

Kāma rasai the?

How is your food?

Vinsanda speaks **SINHALA**.

Assalamo Aleikum.

Hello.

This is Tariq. He speaks **URDU**.

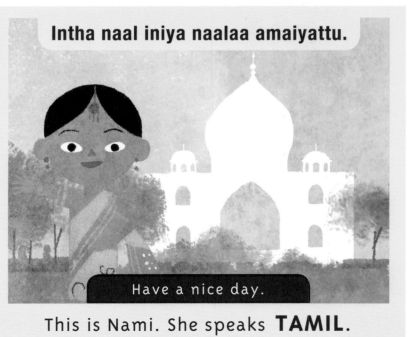

Intha naal iniya naalaa amaiyattu.

Have a nice day.

This is Nami. She speaks **TAMIL**.

Ourakhem hantibel kez.

Pleased to meet you.

Alik speaks **ARMENIAN**.

Shalom.

Hello.

Zev speaks **HEBREW**.

Zama num Malala dhe.

My name is Malala.

This is Malala. She speaks **PASHTO**.

Salaam.

Hello.

Jawid speaks **DARI**.

Esme man Nina.

My name is Nina.

Nina speaks **FARSI**.

Khayr!

Goodbye!

This is Tarana. She speaks **TAJIK**.

Privét!

Hello!

Ochen prijatno.

Pleased to meet you.

This is Sasha.
He speaks **RUSSIAN**.

Namaste.

Hello.

Tapaaiiko naam ke ho?

What's your name.

Mero naam Abhichandra ho.

My name is Abhichandra.

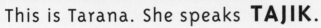

Abhichandra speaks **NEPALI**.

WELCOME TO NORTH & CENTRAL AMERICA

Like South America, languages spoken in North America include a large number of indigenous languages as well as imported languages from Europe and other parts of the world. Many language families are found here—more than one hundred!

Indigenous languages

With more than 500 languages spoken in Central and North America, you might have trouble saying hello to everyone! With geography that spans equatorial regions in Central America to the frozen lands of Alaska and northern Canada, there's a huge amount of variety in the languages that originate here. Whilst we celebrate this diversity today, many native peoples suffered at the hands of European colonizers who sought to take their land and suppress their culture.

Other languages

English, French, and Spanish are the dominant imported languages of the region. English is spoken in the U.S.A. and Canada, French in parts of Canada, and Spanish throughout Mexico and Central America. All of these languages were brought to North and Central America through colonization in the 15th century, when European immigrants brought their cultures and languages with them.

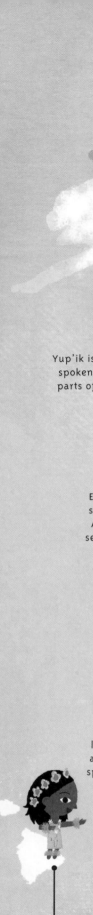

SIOUX LAKOTA
LAKȞÓTIYAPI
Languages belonging to the Sioux family are spoken by more than 30,000 people in North America.

YUP'IK
SUGPIAQ
Yup'ik is an Eskimo language spoken in Alaska (and also parts of Siberia, in Russia!)

NAVAJO
DINÉ BIZAAD
Navajo is widely spoken in southwestern U.S.A. and has more speakers than any other indigenous language on the continent.

ENGLISH
ENGLISH
English is the most widely spoken language in North America thanks to British settlers in the 16th century.

ZUNI
SHIWI'MA
It's not clear what language family Zuni belongs to; it appears to have developed alone for a long, long time. You can find it spoken in Arizona, and New Mexico.

SPANISH
ESPAÑOL
Spanish is the official language in Mexico, and around 40 million people speak it in the U.S.A., too.

TARAHUMARA
RARAMURI
Tarahumara is spoken by about 70,000 people in Mexico.

HAWAIIAN
'ŌLELO HAWAI'I
Hawaii is home to its own language, a Polynesian language related to Maori, Samoan, and Tahitian.

GARIFUNA
KARIF
Garifuna is an Arawak language originally spoken in St Vincent and Dominica, but it spread to South and Central America in the 18th century.

MISKITO
MÍSKITU
Nicaragua and Honduras are home to Miskito.

CREE
NĒHIYAWĒWIN

Canada is home to the Cree language and is an official language of the Northwest Territories.

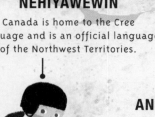

INUKTITUT
ᐃᓄᒃᑎᑐᑦ

Inuktitut is an official language in the north of Canada.

FRENCH
FRANÇAIS

There are more than 2 million French speakers in North America. This language was originally brought over from Europe.

MONTAGNAIS INNU
INNU-AIMUN

Montagnais Innus is an Algonquian language, spoken by more than 10,000 people.

OJIBWE
ANISHINAABEMOWIN

Ojibwe is an Algonquian language spoken in northern parts of the U.S.A. and southern Canada.

SIOUX DAKOTA
DAKOTEYAH

Sioux communities are found in northern U.S.A. states and southern Canadian regions.

NAHUATL
NAUATL

There are many languages belonging to the Nahuatl family, which also used to be known as Aztec.

CHEROKEE
TSALAGI GAWONIHISDI

Cherokee is considered a difficult language to learn, with very long words compared to English.

PUREPECHA
P'URHEPECHA

Purepecha is also known as Tarascan. It's a language isolate—it's not clear which family it belongs to.

OTOMI
HÑÄHÑU

Otomi is a tonal language spoken in central Mexico.

CHINANTEC
JU JMÍI

Chinantec is a tonal language, so its meaning can change if the speaker alters their pitch.

CHOCTAW
CHAHTA

Choctaaw is a Muscogean language spoken in southeastern U.S.A.

MAZAHUA
JÑATRJO

Mazahua is a Mesoamerican language found in parts of central Mexico.

HAITIAN CREOLE
KREYÒL

Haitian Creole is a blend of French and African languages. All creole languages grow from contact between an introduced language and an indigenous one.

YUCATEC MAYA
MÀAYA T'ÀAN

Travel to Belize or the Yucatan Peninsula to hear Yucatan Maya spoken.

DUTCH
NEDERLANDS

Dutch is spoken in Suriname, Aruba, Curaçao, and Sint Maarten.

MIXE
AYUUJK

Head to southern Mexico to practice saying hello in Zoque!

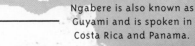

NGÄBERE
KUGUE NGABERE

Ngabere is also known as Guyami and is spoken in Costa Rica and Panama.

PAPIAMENTO
PAPIAMENTU

Papiamento is also a creole language, spoken in the Caribbean. Its roots lie in Portuguese and African languages.

ZAPOTEK
DIIDXAZÁ

Zapotec is spoken in parts of Mexico, though there are a few dialects. Accents and vocabulary can vary from place to place.

Il fait froid!

It's cold!

This is Elodie. She speaks **FRENCH**.

Hallo!

Hello!

Kiitos!

Mijn naam is Calvin.

This is Calvin.
He speaks **DUTCH**.

¿Cómo te llamas?

What's your name?

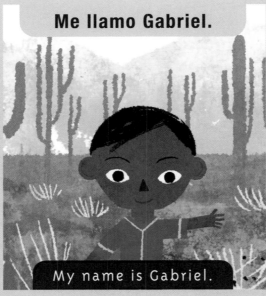

Me llamo Gabriel.

My name is Gabriel.

Adiós!

Bye!

This is Gabriel. He speaks **SPANISH**.

Xacza.

Hello.

Lluan speaks **ZAPOTEK**.

Ma thuhu Maria.

My name is Maria.

Maria speaks **OTOMI**.

Najotj'o ri nzengwats'ü.

Pleased to meet you.

This is Lupe. She speaks **MAZAHUA**.

E ju xá.

Hello.

¿A dxúnno?

How are you?

Jné dxúnna.

I'm fine.

This is Péen. He speaks **CHINANTEC**.

Buiti binafin.

Good morning.

Buiti Bóustarun Irumu!

Happy birthday!

This is Ara. She speaks **GARIFUNA.**

Ti mxëë?

What's your name?

Ana speaks **MIXE.**

Kuiraba.

Hello.

Chu niri?

How are you?

This is Luiwisi. He speaks **TARAHUMARA.**

Ngantore!

Hello!

Mego speaks **NGÄBERE.**

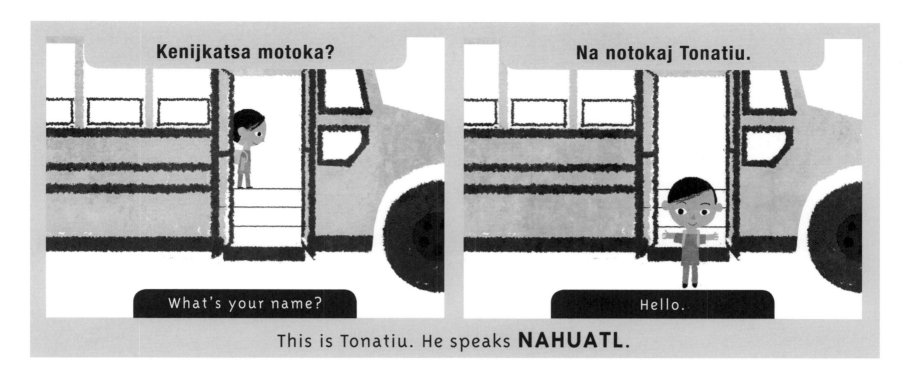

Kenijkatsa motoka?

What's your name?

Na notokaj Tonatiu.

Hello.

This is Tonatiu. He speaks **NAHUATL**.

Nare chuskuki.

Hello.

Behind this mask is Tsïtsïki! She speaks **PUREPECHA**.

Yang ninam lika Jose.

My name is Jose.

Jose speaks **MISKITO**.

Hau'oli kēia hui 'ana o kāua.

Pleased to meet you.

Ailani speaks **HAWAIIAN**.

35

Ki'htwa'm kawa'pamitin.

Pleased to meet you.

Ta'nisi?

How are you?

M'ona na'ntaw.

I'm fine.

This is Hurit. She speaks **CREE**.

Kuei.

Hello.

Mashku speaks **MONTAGNAIS INNU**.

Aaniin ezhinikaazoyan?

What's your name?

Leona speaks **OJIBWE**.

Quviagijara Paco.

My name is Paco.

Paco speaks **INUKTITUT**.

Ya'at'eeh.

Hello.

Baa hozhoogo Nidizhchi!

Happy birthday!

This is Nizhoni. She speaks **NAVAJO**.

Doka.

See you later.

This is Sunktokeca. He speaks **SIOUX DAKOTA**.

Haw.

Hi.

This is Dyani. She speaks **SIOUX LAKOTA**.

Keshhi.

Hello.

Ko' do' dewanan deyaye?

How are you?

This is Meli. She speaks **ZUNI**.

Osiyo.

Hello.

Donadagvhoi.

Goodbye.

This is Adsila. She speaks **CHEROKEE**.

Bon apeti!

Enjoy your meal!

This is Astryd. She speaks **HAITIAN CREOLE**

Contento di mira bo.

Pleased to meet you.

Maudrith speaks **PAPIAMENTO**.

Halito!

Hello!

Nitushi speaks **CHOCTAW**.

WELCOME TO SOUTH AMERICA

There are almost 450 indigenous languages spoken in South America, alongside languages from around the world that have arrived through centuries of colonization and trade. Portuguese and Spanish are the most spoken non-indigenous languages, but you can also find others like Japanese and Arabic.

Indigenous languages

The 450 languages of South America are divided into 37 language families. This amazing diversity comes in part from the extreme geography of South America. Mighty rivers and the enormous Andes meant communities developed over hundreds and thousands of years in isolation, preserving languages from contact and influence with others.

European languages

Spanish, or Castellano (as it is called in South America), and Portuguese arrived in South America around the 15th century, and war and colonization cemented their role in South American life. During this period, thousands of European people immigrated to South America, and sought to take power and dominate the indigenous people (those who already lived there) with their own culture and language. Other European languages also took root in this fashion, including Dutch, French, and English.

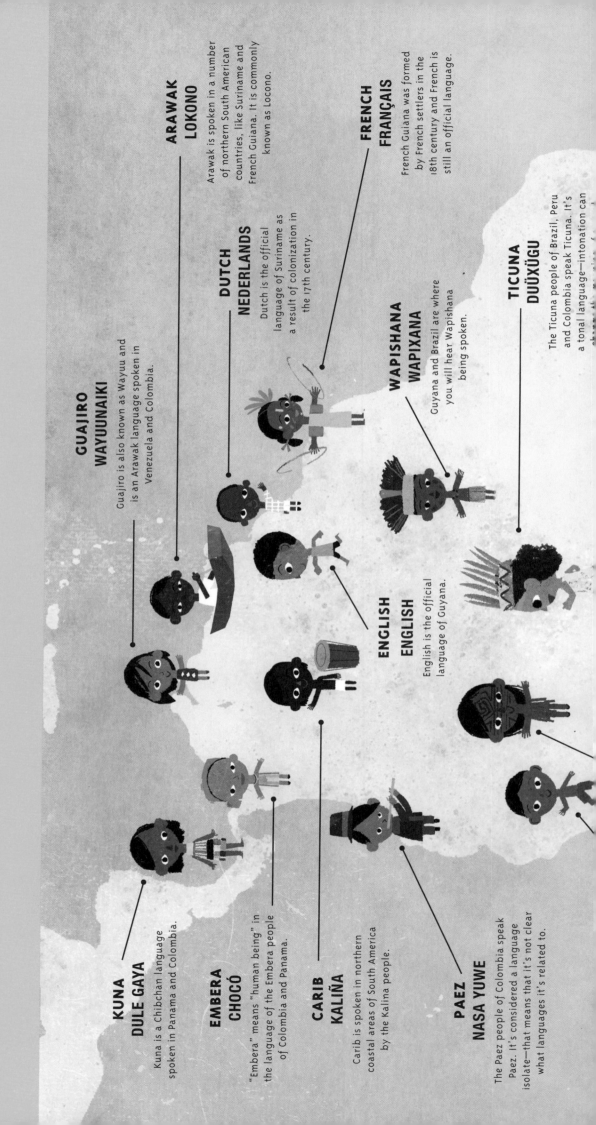

ARAWAK
LOKONO

Arawak is spoken in a number of northern South American countries, like Suriname and French Guiana. It is commonly known as Locono.

FRENCH
FRANÇAIS

French Guiana was formed by French settlers in the 18th century and French is still an official language.

DUTCH
NEDERLANDS

Dutch is the official language of Suriname as a result of colonization in the 17th century.

TICUNA
DUÜXÜGU

The Ticuna people of Brazil, Peru and Colombia speak Ticuna. It's a tonal language—intonation can change the meaning [...]

WAPISHANA
WAPIXANA

Guyana and Brazil are where you will hear Wapishana being spoken.

GUAJIRO
WAYUUNAIKI

Guajiro is also known as Wayuu and is an Arawak language spoken in Venezuela and Colombia.

ENGLISH
ENGLISH

English is the official language of Guyana.

KUNA
DULE GAYA

Kuna is a Chibchan language spoken in Panama and Colombia.

EMBERA
CHOCÓ

"Embera" means "human being" in the language of the Embera people of Colombia and Panama.

CARIB
KALIÑA

Carib is spoken in northern coastal areas of South America by the Kalina people.

PAEZ
NASA YUWE

The Paez people of Colombia speak Paez. It's considered a language isolate—that means that it's not clear what languages it's related to.

BRAZILIAN PORTUGUESE
BRASILEIRO

As you can guess, Brazilian Portuguese is spoken in Brazil, because of the Portuguese who colonized the region in 16th century. It has the largest number of speakers of any language in South America.

GUARANI
YVYPÓRA RÉRA

Guarani is one of the official languages of Paraguay and one of the most popularly spoken languages of South America. You can also hear it in neighboring parts of Argentina, Bolivia, and Brazil.

AYMARA
AYMAR ARU

Aymara, like Quechua, is spoken in the Andes.

SPANISH (CASTELLANO)
ESPAÑOL

Spanish is spoken as the national language of most countries in South America. Each country speaks its own version—some words are different and accents change as well.

QUECHUA
KECHUA

Quechua is the most widely spoken indigenous language in South America, spoken predominantly in the Andes.

MAPUNDUNGUN
BREZHONEG

The Mapuche people speak Mapudungun in their home area of Galvarino, Chile, and western Argentina.

ASHANINKA
ASHANINKA

Travel to the rainforests of Peru to practice your Ashaninka language!

YINE
YINE

Yine is spoken in Peru, in areas around the Ucayali River. Around 4,000 people speak this language.

WIZNAY
OKHAJ LHICH

Wiznay is spoken in Argentina by people who live near the Pilcomayo River.

This is Elodie. She speaks **FRENCH**.

Fleur speaks **DUTCH**.

This is Ezra. He speaks **ENGLISH**.

Amh'te na.

Hello.

Olhey thad.

My name is Olhey.

This is Olhey. He speaks **WIZNAY**.

Avy'aite roikuaávo.

Pleased to meet you.

This is Jacy. She speaks **GUARANI**.

Klo giwakyi?

What is your name?

Ngiwakni Rittma.

My name is Rittma.

This is Rittma.
She speaks **YINE**.

Imaynallan kashanki?

How are you?

This is Izhi. She speaks **QUECHUA**.

Mari mari pichi keche.

Hello.

Ayuwi tañi puike.

Pleased to meet you.

This is Elvira.
He speaks **MAPUDUNGUN**.

Kamisaki.

Hello.

Kunjamaskatasa?

How are you?

Hualiquithua.

I'm fine.

This is Severino. He speaks **AYMARA**.

Ma wa Otoidanibo.

My name is Otoidanibo.

Otoidanibo speaks **CARIB**.

Kaiman?

How are you?

Oo, kaiman.

I'm fine.

This is Masiki.
She speaks **WAPISHANA**.

Mena.

Hello.

This is Maria. She speaks **EMBERA**.

Boili halakoba.

Hello.

This is Sabantho. He speaks ARAWAK.

Ewcha.

Hello.

Ma'ucha?

How are you?

This is Avirama.
He speaks **PAEZ**.

Nacabe.

Hello.

Naka nopaita, Tsitsire.

My name is Tsitsire.

Kametsa ayotabaka.

Pleased to meet you.

Tsitsire speaks **ASHANINKA**.

Numae.

Hello.

Takui kuega?

What's your name?

Chauega nii.

My name is Chauega.

Chauega speaks TICUNA.

Na.

Hello.

This is Luisa. She speaks **KUNA**.

Anayaasüje pia?

How are you?

Anasü taya.

I'm fine.

This is Tanulia. She speaks GUAJIRO.

WELCOME TO AFRICA

There are about 2,000 languages spoken in Africa: what a journey from top to bottom it is! From the north where Semitic languages like Arabic and Amharic are spoken, through the great plains where you encounter Nilo-Saharan languages, to the south where colonization left Dutch to become Afrikaans and live beside indigenous languages like Zulu and Swahili.

Niger-Congo languages
This is Africa's largest language family and runs through the middle of the continent to the south. Yoruba, Igbo, Fula, Shona, and Zulu all belong to this family.

Afroasiatic languages
This family contains around 300 languages and dialects, spoken predominantly in North Africa and the Horn of Africa. The most well known Afroasiatic language is probably Arabic, but Hausa, Amharic and Somali also belong to this family.

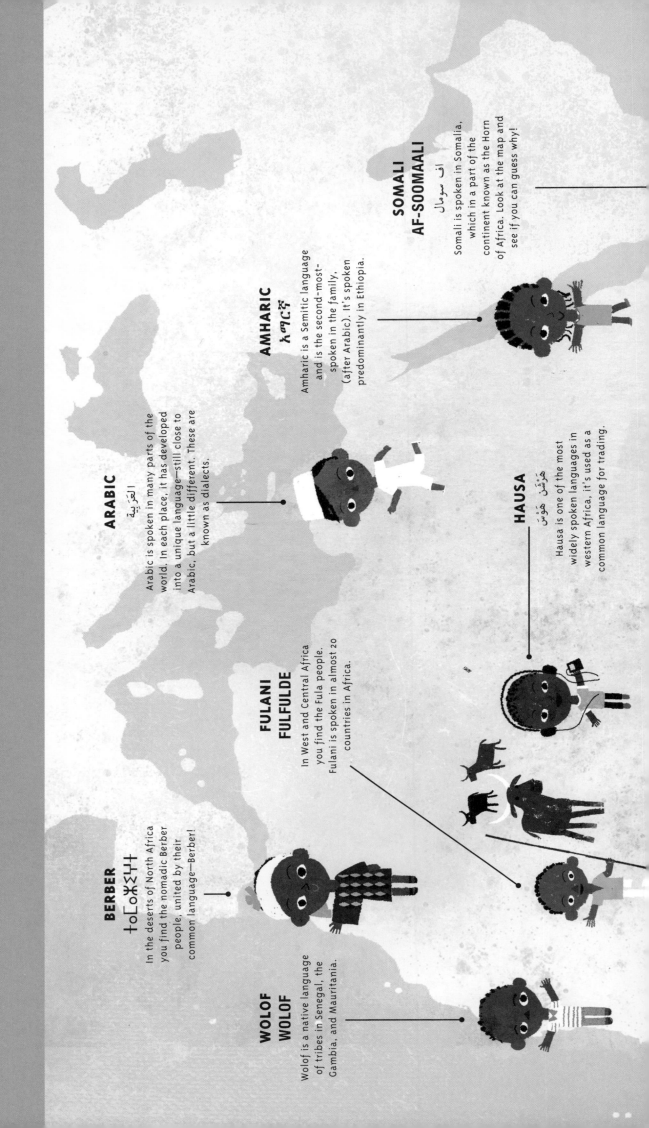

SOMALI
AF-SOOMAALI
اف سومالي
Somali is spoken in Somalia, which in a part of the continent known as the Horn of Africa. Look at the map and see if you can guess why!

AMHARIC
አማርኛ
Amharic is a Semitic language and is the second-most-spoken in the family, (after Arabic). It's spoken predominantly in Ethiopia.

ARABIC
العربية
Arabic is spoken in many parts of the world. In each place, it has developed into a unique language—still close to Arabic, but a little different. These are known as dialects.

HAUSA
هَرْشَن هَوْسَ
Hausa is one of the most widely spoken languages in western Africa, it's used as a common language for trading.

FULANI
FULFULDE
In West and Central Africa you find the Fula people. Fulani is spoken in almost 20 countries in Africa.

BERBER
ⵜⴰⵎⴰⵣⵉⵖⵜ
In the deserts of North Africa you find the nomadic Berber people, united by their common language—Berber!

WOLOF
WOLOF
Wolof is a native language of tribes in Senegal, the Gambia, and Mauritania.

OROMO
AFAAN OROMOO

Ethiopia is home to a number of languages, one of which is Oromo.

CHICHEWA
CHICHEWA

This language is also known as Chewa. It's the most widely spoken language in Malawi.

MALAGASY
MALAGASY

Malagasy is the language of Madagascar, an island off the coast of Africa.

IGBO
ASỤSỤ IGBO

The Igbo people of Nigeria speak this language. It's a tonal language which means the pitch you use when saying a word can change the meaning.

SWAHILI
KISWAHILI

Swahili is sometimes called Kiswahili. It's the national language of four African countries—Tanzania, Kenya, Uganda, and the Democratic Republic of the Congo.

ZULU
ISIZULU

Zulu, or isiZulu as it's sometimes known, is spoken in South Africa and is one of 11 official languages there.

YORUBA
ÈDÈ YORÙBÁ

Yoruba is another language spoken in Nigeria. It is the most widely spoken African language outside of Africa.

PORTUGUESE
PORTUGUÊS

Portuguese is the official language of six African countries—Angola, Mozambique, Guinea-Bissau, Cape Verde, São Tomé and Principe, and Equatorial Guinea.

SHONA
SHONA

The Shona people of Zimbabwe speak Shona and it is an official language in that country.

AFRIKAANS
BREZHONEG

Afrikaans, spoken in southern Africa, is known as a "daughter language"—Dutch is its parent. They are very closely related!

FRENCH
FRANÇAIS

Around 120 million people speak French in Africa. This is because the French colonized a number of African countries.

ENGLISH
ENGLISH

English was brought to Africa from Europe during colonial times and is still spoken in parts of eastern, western and southern Africa.

TSWANA
SETSWANA

Tswana is an official language of Botswana, though the majority of speakers are in South Africa.

This is Amal. He speaks **SOMALI**.

This is Amaziy. He speaks **BERBER**.

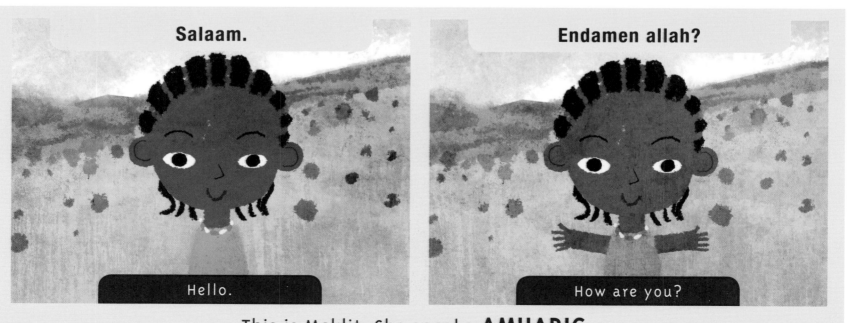

This is Meklit. She speaks **AMHARIC**.

53

Akaam.

Hello.

Akam Jirtuu?

How are you?

Fayya.

I'm fine.

This is Meti. She speaks **OROMO**.

Sannu.

Hello.

Sey yeso.

Goodbye.

This is Bari. He speaks **FULANI**.

Gini bu aha gi?

What's your name?

Aham bu Ebele.

My name is Ebele.

This is Ebele.
She speaks **IGBO**.

This is Abeni. She speaks **YORUBA**.

This is Karel.
He speaks **AFRIKAANS**.

This is Pierre. He speaks **FRENCH**.

Sannu.

Hello.

Kina lafiya?

How are you?

This is Azumi. He speaks **HAUSA**.

Manao ahoana.

Hello!

Felana speaks **MALAGASY**.

Ola!

Hi!

De onde você é?

Where are you from?

This is Paula. She speaks **PORTUGUESE**.

Ndafara kukuzivai.

Pleased to meet you,

This is Maita. She speaks **SHONA**.

Salamou Alaykoum.

Hello.

Na nga def?

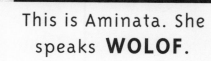

How are you?

This is Aminata. She
speaks **WOLOF**.

Sawubona.

Hello.

Ngiyajabula ukukwazi.

Pleased to meet you.

Lo ngumfowethu.

This is my brother.

This is Langa. He speaks **ZULU**.

Hello.

Pleased to meet you.

My name is Bruce.

Hello.

Pleased to meet you.

My name is Bruce.

Bruce speaks **ENGLISH**.

Muli bwanji?

How are you?

This is Thoko. She speaks **CHICHEWA**.

Dumela.

Le kae?

Hello.

How are you?

This is Kgosi. He speaks **TSWANA**.

WELCOME TO OCEANIA

While English has become the dominant language of Oceania, there are hundreds of other languages spoken throughout the region. From other imported languages, like French, to the large number of indigenous languages in Australia, and the Polynesian languages in the Pacific, you can find them all here in Oceania.

Australian languages

When Europeans first arrived to Australia there were between 500 and 700 languages spoken by indigenous people. The majority of these languages have died with about 150 languages still in use, though many of these have just a few speakers left. Most Australian languages belong to the Pama—Nyungan family.

Polynesian languages

There are around 40 Polynesian languages and it can be quite easy to see or hear similarities. You might notice some when you look at the words in this book. These Pacific island languages have lent a number of words to English—like "taboo" and "ukulele."

TAGALOG
WIKANG TAGALOG
Tagalog is also known as Filipino, so you can probably guess where it's commonly spoken— the Philippines!

TOK PISIN
TOK PISIN
This language is spoken in Papua New Guinea, and evolved from English brought by travelers—"Tok" comes from the English word, "Talk."

TIWI
TIWI
Tiwi is a language isolate spoken on a small island just off the coast of northern Australia.

WARLPIRI
WARLPIRI
Warlpiri is spoken in the Northern Territory of Australia by around 3,000 people.

AUSTRALIAN KRIOL
KRIOL
Australian Kriol grew out of a blend of indigenous languages, English, and other immigrant languages found in Australia.

ARRERNTE
ARRERNTE
Travel to the centre of Australia and the deserts around Alice Springs to find this indigenous Australian language.

ENGLISH
ENGLISH
English arrived in Australia in the late 18th century, when the British established settlements on the continent.

HAWAIIAN
'ŌLELO HAWAI'I

Hawaii is home to its own
language, a Polynesian
language related to Maori,
Samoan and Tahitian.

FIJIAN
NA VOSA VAKAVITI

Fijian is a Polynesian language
and one of three official
languages of Fiji, alongside
English, and Hindi.

SAMOAN
GAGANA FA'A SĀMOA

Samoan is a Polynesian
language spoken in Polynesia.

YOLNGU
YOLNGU MATHA

The northeastern tip of Arnhem
land in Australia is home to
Yolngu.

TONGAN
LEA FAKA-TONGA

Tongan is the national
language of Tonga. It's a
Polynesian language as well.

FRENCH
FRANÇAIS

French is spoken in a
number of Polynesian
states including Tahiti
and New Caledonia.

TAHITIAN
REO TAHITI

The paradise of islands
that is Tahiti is home
to one of the dominant
languages of Polynesia.

MAORI
TE REO MĀORI

Maori is an official language
of New Zealand, alongside
English.

61

Bula!

Hi.

Vacava tiko?

How are you?

Bula Bula Vinaka Tiko.

I'm fine.

This is Sereano. She speaks **FIJIAN**.

Werte.

Hello.

Leshay speaks **ARRERNTE**.

Bon anniversaire!

Happy birthday!

Michel speaks **FRENCH**.

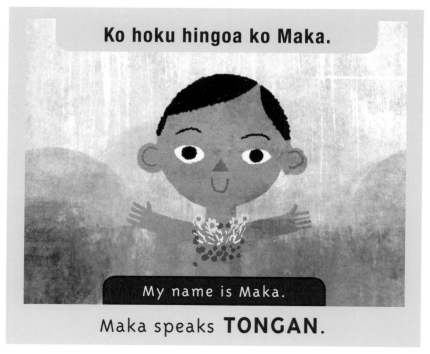

Ko hoku hingoa ko Maka.

My name is Maka.

Maka speaks **TONGAN**.

Rachel speaks **ENGLISH**.

This is Ali. He speaks
AUSTRALIAN KRIOL.

This is Talia. She speaks **SAMOAN**.

E aha tō 'oe huru?

How are you?

Maita'i.

I'm fine.

This is Manuia. She speaks **TAHITIAN**.

Magandang araw sa'yo!

Have a good day!

This is Shirley. She speaks **TAGALOG**.

Yuwa.

Hello.

Ngakarnangku nyanyi.

See you later.

This is Japaljarri.
He speaks **WARLPIRI**.

Hai!

Hi!

Yu stap gut?

How are you?

Mi stap gut.

I'm fine.

This is Mekere. He speaks **TOK PISIN**.

Awungana!

Hello!

This is Bede. She speaks **TIWI**.

Makarr yun gumurr yun nhe.

Pleased to meet you.

Bubu.

Goodbye.

This is Binmila. She speaks **YOLNGU**.

WELCOME TO ANTARCTICA

The family of languages spoken on Antarctica is an interesting one. The main thing they have in common is they're all spoken in Antarctica!

Antarctica was first sighted by Russian explorers about 200 years ago. Strangely, the name for this ice-covered continent was proposed almost 2,000 years ago! It means "opposite of the arctic"—scholars like Aristotle had long believed there would be a cold icy land to balance what they knew as the Arctic.

In Antarctica today you'll find an enormous number of languages being spoken—a result of the wide range of researchers who visit Antarctica to study the frozen land. Seven countries have staked a claim on parts of Antarctica and 30 countries have research stations there.

NORWEGIAN NORSK

Queen Maud Land is a part of the continent claimed by Norway.

SWEDISH SVENSKA

Swedish stations in Antarctica have set up programs that monitor the environment.

ENGLISH ENGLISH

English is by far the most spoken language on Antarctica, with people from Australia, the United Kingdom, the U.S.A., Canada, New Zealand and South Africa there all year round.

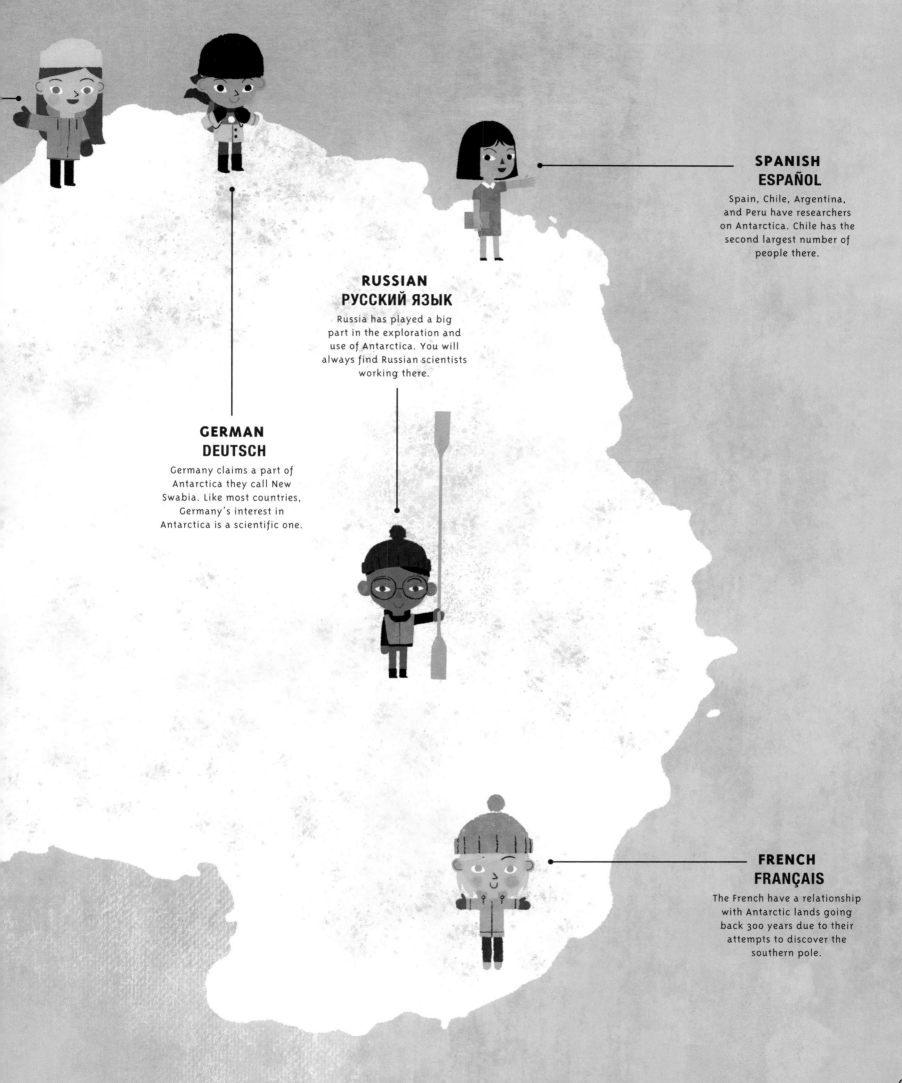

SPANISH
ESPAÑOL

Spain, Chile, Argentina, and Peru have researchers on Antarctica. Chile has the second largest number of people there.

RUSSIAN
РУССКИЙ ЯЗЫК

Russia has played a big part in the exploration and use of Antarctica. You will always find Russian scientists working there.

GERMAN
DEUTSCH

Germany claims a part of Antarctica they call New Swabia. Like most countries, Germany's interest in Antarctica is a scientific one.

FRENCH
FRANÇAIS

The French have a relationship with Antarctic lands going back 300 years due to their attempts to discover the southern pole.

My name is Zack.

My name is Zack.

I'm cold!

I'm cold.

This is Zack. He speaks **ENGLISH**.

Je m'appelle Marie.

My name is Marie.

Marie speaks **FRENCH**.

Hej!

Hello!

Hur är det?

How are you?

This is Elin. She speaks **SWEDISH**.

70

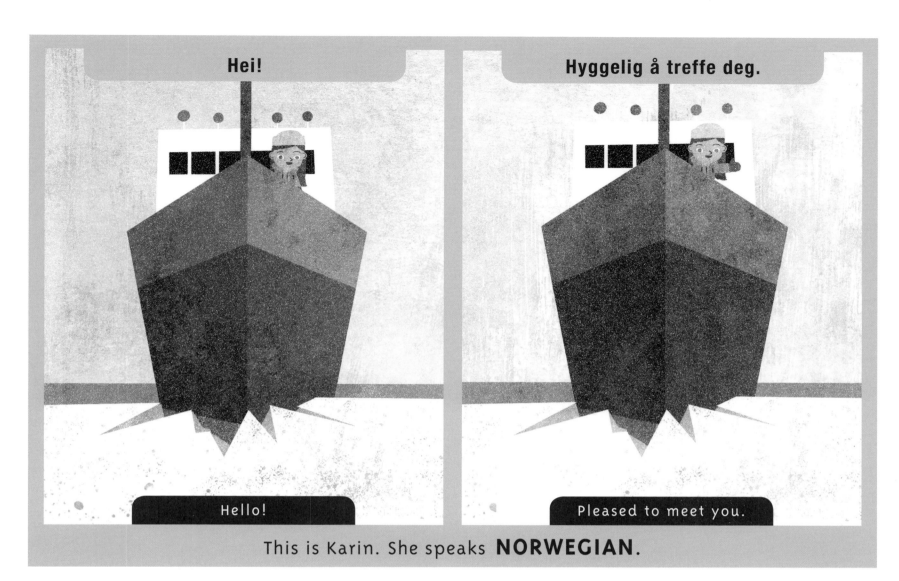

This is Karin. She speaks **NORWEGIAN**.

This is Raquel. She speaks **SPANISH**.

FURTHER PHRASES

EUROPE

FRENCH
Bonjour.	Hello.
Comment vas-tu?	How are you?
Bien!	I'm fine!
Enchantée!	Pleased to meet you!
Comment tu t'appelle?	What's your name?
Je m'appelle Pierre.	My name is Pierre.
Bon anniversaire!	Happy Birthday!

ITALIAN
Ciao!	Hello!
Come stai?	How are you?
Bene!	I'm fine!
Piacere.	Pleased to meet you.
Come ti chiami.	What's your name?
Mi chiamo Maria.	My name is Maria.
Grazie.	Thank you.

SPANISH
¡Hola!	Hello!
¿Cómo estás?	How are you?
Bien!	I'm fine!
Encantado.	Pleased to meet you.
¿Cómo te llamas?	What's your name?
Me llamo Santiago.	My name is Santiago.
¡Qué día tan bonito!	It's a beautiful day!

ROMANIAN
Bună ziua.	Good day.
Ce mai faci?	How are you?
Bine.	I'm fine.
Încântat de cunoștință.	Pleased to meet you.
Cum vă numiți?	What's your name?
Numele meu este Adriana.	My name is Adriana.

PORTUGUESE
Olá.	Hello.
Como estás?	How are you?
Estou bem.	I'm fine.
Prazer em conhecer-te.	Pleased to meet you.
Como te chamas?	What's your name?
O meu nome é João.	My name is Joao.
Tem um bom dia.	Have a good day.

SWEDISH
Hej!	Hello!
Hur är det?	How are you?
Bra.	I'm fine.
Trevligt att träffas.	Pleased to meet you.
Vad heter du?	What's your name?
Jag heter Alice.	My name is Alice.
Var kommer du ifrån?	Where do you come from?

CATALAN
Hola!	Hello!
Com està?	How are you?
Bé.	I'm fine.
Tant de gust.	Pleased to meet you.
Com et dius?	What's your name?
Em dic Caterina.	My name is Caterina.
Bon profit!	Enjoy your meal!

GERMAN
Guten Tag!	Hello!
Wie geht's?	How are you?
Gut.	I'm fine.
Schön, dich kennen zu lernen.	Pleased to meet you.
Wie heißt du?	What's your name?
Ich heiße Felix.	My name is Felix.
Auf Wiedersehen.	Goodbye.

DUTCH
Hallo!	Hello!
Hoe gaat het?	How are you?
Goed.	I'm fine.
Wat is jouw naam?	What's your name?
Mijn naam is Isa.	My name is Isa.
Fijne Verjaardag!	Happy birthday!
Tot ziens.	See you later.

ENGLISH
Hello!	Hello!
How are you?	How are you?
I'm fine.	I'm fine.
Pleased to meet you.	Pleased to meet you.
What's your name?	What's your name?
My name is George.	My name is George.
It's a beautiful day!	It's a beautiful day!

DANISH
Hej!	Hello!
Hvordan har du det?	How are you?
Fint.	I'm fine.
Rart at møde dig.	Pleased to meet you.
Hvad hedder du?	What's your name?
Jeg hedder Freja	My name is Freja.
God rejse!	Have a good trip!

NORWEGIAN
Hei!	Hello!
Hvordan har du det?	How are you?
Takk, bare bra.	I'm fine.
Hyggelig å treffe deg.	Pleased to meet you.
Hva heter du?	What's your name?
Jeg heter Svein.	My name is Svein.
Jeg er fra Oslo.	I'm from Oslo.

ICELANDIC
Halló!	Hello!
Hvað segir þú?	How are you?
Allt got.	I'm fine.
Gaman að hitta þig.	Pleased to meet you.
Hvað heitirðu?	What's your name?
Ég heiti Bjork.	My name is Bjork.
Hafðu það gott.	Have a nice day.

FINNISH
Hei!	Hello!
Mitä kuuluu?	How are you?
Kiitos hyvin.	I'm fine.
Hauska tavata.	Pleased to meet you.
Mikä sun nimi on?	What's your name?
Mun nimi on Mikko.	My name is Mikko.
Heippa.	Goodbye.

RUSSIAN
Privét!	Hello!
Kak delá?	How are you?
Horosho.	I'm fine.
Ochen prijatno.	Pleased to meet you.
Kak teb'a zovut?	What's your name?
Men'a zovut Anastasia.	My name is Anastasia.
Prijatnovo appetita!	Enjoy your meal!

POLISH
Cześć.	Hello.
Jak się masz?	How are you?
Dobrze!	I'm fine.
Miło mi.	Pleased to meet you.
Jak masz na imię?	What's your name?
Mam na imię Artur.	My name is Arthur.
Dziękuję.	Thank you.

SERBIAN
Zdravo!	Hello!
Kako ste?	How are you?
Hvala!	I'm fine.
Drago mi je.	Pleased to meet you.
Kako se zovete?	What's your name?
Zovem se Nada.	My name is Nada.
Doviđenja.	Goodbye.

WELSH
Helô!	Hello!
Syd wyt ti?	How are you?
Dwi'n iawn.	I'm fine.
Neis cyfarfod efo chdi.	Pleased to meet you.
Beth ydy dy enw di?	What's your name?
Tomos dwi.	My name is Tomos.
Dwi'n dod o Sir Fôn.	I'm from Anglesey.

HUNGARIAN
Szia!	Hi!
Hogy vagy?	How are you?
Jól.	I'm fine.
Örvendek.	Pleased to meet you.
Hogy hívnak?	What's your name?
Eszter vagyok.	My name is Eszter.
Viszlát.	Goodbye.

LATVIAN
Labdien!	Hello!
Kā tev iet?	How are you?
Man iet labi.	I'm fine.
Priecājos ar tevi iepazīties.	Pleased to meet you.
Kā tevi sauc?	What's your name?
Mani sauc Karlis.	My name is Karlis.
Paldies.	Thank you.

LITHUANIAN
Labas.	Hi.
Kaip gyveni?	How are you?
Gerai!	I'm fine!
Malonu susipažinti.	Pleased to meet you.
Koks tavo vardas?	What's your name?
Mano vardas Elgé.	My name is Elgé.
Su gimtadieniu.	Happy birthday.

BRETON
Demat.	Hello.
Mat an traoù?	How are you?
Ya, mat-tre.	I'm fine.
Laouen on da gejañ ganit.	Pleased to meet you.
Petra eo da anv?	What's your name?
Yann eo ma anv.	My name is Yann.
Deiz-ha-bloaz laouen.	Happy birthday.

GAELIC

Dia duit. — Hello.
Conas atá tú? — How are you?
Tá mé go maith. — I'm fine.
Tá áthas orm buaileadh leat. — Pleased to meet you.
Cad is ainm duit? — What's your name?
Máire is ainm dom. — My name is Máire.
Go raibh maith agat. — Thank you.

CROATIAN

Bok. — Hello.
Kako si? — How are you?
Dobro! — I'm fine!
Drago mi je. — Pleased to meet you.
Kako se zoveš? — What's your name?
Zovem se Josip. — My name is Josip.
Odakle si? — Where are you from?

SLOVAK

Ahoj. — Hello.
Ako sa máš? — How are you?
Dobre! — I'm fine!
Teší ma. — Pleased to meet you.
Ako sa voláš? — What's your name?
Volám sa Andrej. — My name is Andrej.
Všetko najlepšie! — Happy birthday!

CZECH

Dobrý den! — Hello!
Jak se máš? — How are you?
Mám se dobře. — I'm fine.
Těší mě. — Pleased to meet you.
Jak se jmenuješ? — What's your name?
Jmenuji se Ivona. — My name is Ivona.
Na viděnou. — See you later.

GREEK

Ya su! — Hello!
Pos íse? — How are you?
Kala! — I'm fine.
Hárika. — Pleased to meet you.
Pós se léne? — What's your name?
Me léne Ajax. — My name is Ajax.
Kaló taksídi! — Have a good journey!

TURKISH

Merhaba. — Hello.
Nasılsın? — How are you?
İyiyim. — I'm fine.
Memnun oldum. — Pleased to meet you.
Adın ne? — What's your name?
Adım Reyyan. — My name is Reyyan.
Sonra görüşürüz. — See you later.

ASIA

THAI

Sa-wat-dee. — Hello.
Sabaai dee mai? — How are you?
Sabaai dee ka. — I'm fine (girl speaking).
Yin dee tee dai roo jak. — Pleased to meet you.
Kun chue a-rai? — What's your name?
Pom chue Nam. — My name is Nam.
Wat dee! — Bye!

INDONESIAN

Halo. — Hello.
Apa kabar? — How are you?
Baik, terima kasih. — I'm fine.
Senang bertemu dengan Anda. — Pleased to meet you.
Namamu siapa? — What's your name?
Nama saya Intan. — My name is Intan.
Selamat tinggal! — Bye!

MALAY

Selamat datang. — Hello.
Apa khabar? — How are you?
Khabar baik. — I'm fine.
Selamat berkenalan. — Pleased to meet you.
Siapa nama anda? — What's your name?
Nama saya Syukri. — My name is Syukri.
Jumpa Lagi. — See you later.

TAGALOG

Musta. — Hello.
Kumusta ka? — How are you?
Mabuti naman. — I'm fine.
Kinagagalak kong makilala ka. — Pleased to meet you.
Anong pangalan mo? — What's your name?
Ako si Amihan. — My name is Amihan.
Magandang araw sa'yo! — Have a good day!

KHMER

Johm riab sua. — Hello.
Niak sohk sabaay te? — How are you?
Knyohm sohk sabaay. — I'm fine.
Khnyom trawk aw naa dael baan skoal loak. — Pleased to meet you.
Neak chmuah ay? — What's your name?
Knyohm chmuah Sok. — My name is Sok.
Mien tingay la-aw. — Have a nice day.

BURMESE

Mingala pa. — Hello.
Nei kaon la? — How are you?
Nekaunbade. — I'm fine.
Thin nai twai ya da wan thar ba de. — Pleased to meet you.
Thint nan me be lo khaw tha le? — What's your name?
Ja ma nau na me Thiri ba. — My name is Thiri.
Mwe nay mingala pa. — Happy birthday.

VIETNAMESE

Xin chao. — Hello.
Ban co khoe khong? — How are you?
Khoe. — I'm fine.
Rat vui duoc gap ban. — Pleased to meet you.
Ban den gi? — What's your name?
Toi den la Linh. — My name is Linh.
Chuc mung nam moi! — Happy New Year!

CANTONESE

Neih hou. — Hello.
Neih hou ma. — How are you?
Hou. — I'm fine.
Hahng wuih. — Pleased to meet you.
Neih dim chingfu a? — What's your name?
Ngoh giujouh Tai. — My name is Tai.

JAPANESE

Konnichiwa. — Hello.
O genki desu ka? — How are you?
Hajimemashite. — Pleased to meet you.
O-namae wa nan desu ka? — What's your name?
Watashi no name wa Yukiko desu. — My name is Yukiko.
Otanjōbi omedetō gozaimasu. — Happy birthday.

MANDARIN

Ni hao. — Hello.
Ni hao ma? — How are you?
Wǒ hěn hǎo. — I'm fine.
Hen gaoxing renshi ni. — Pleased to meet you.
Nǐ jiào shénme míngzi? — What's your name?
Wo jiao Feng. — My name is Feng.
Zàijiàn. — Goodbye.

KOREAN

Annyeong haseyo. — Hello.
Eotteoke jinaeyo? — How are you?
Jal jinaeyo. — I'm fine.
Mannaseo bangaweoyo. — Pleased to meet you.
Ireumi meoyeyo? — What's your name?
Nae ireumeun Okkyun iyeyo. — My name is Okkyun.
Gomaweoyo. — Thank you.

LAO

Sabaai-dii! — Hello!
Sabaai-dii baw? — How are you?
Khawy sabaai-dii. — I'm fine.
Dii jai thii huu kap jao. — Pleased to meet you.
Jâo Suu Nyung? — What's your name?
Khawy seu Konala. — My name is Konala.
Khaw thoht. — Excuse me.

BENGALI

Nomoshkar. — Hello.
Apni kemon achen? — How are you?
Ami bhalo achi. — I'm fine.
Apnar shathe alap hoe khub bhalo laglo. — Pleased to meet you.
Apnar naam ki? — What's your name?
Amar nam Sujit. — My name is Sujit.
Apnar din bhalo katu! — Have a nice day!

SINHALA

Ayubuvan. — Hello.
Kohomadha? — How are you?
Hondhin innava. — I'm fine.
Muta asahi oyawa hambaunata. — Pleased to meet you.
Oyaage nama mokakdha? — What's your name?
Mage nama Vinsanda. — My name is Vinsanda.
Kāma rasai the? — How is your food?

URDU

Assalamo Aleikum. — Hello.
Kya hal hai? — How are you?
Main theek hun. — I'm fine.
Aap se milker khushi huwi! — Pleased to meet you!
Aapka nam kya hai? — What's your name?
Mera Naam Hai Tariq. — My name is Tariq.
Shaam Bukhair. — Good evening.

TAMIL

Vanakkam. — Hello.
Eppadi irukkīnga? — How are you?
Nalam! — I'm fine!
Ongalaa paaththadhu rumba sandhoshaa. — Pleased to meet you.
Ung ga per enna? — What's your name?
Em per Nami. — My name is Nami.
Intha naal iniya naalaa amaiyattu. — Have a nice day.

HINDI

Namaste. — Hello.
Sab achha hai? — How are you?
Mai thik hu. — I'm fine.
Ap se milkar khushi hui. — Pleased to meet you.
Apka nam kya hai? — What's your name?
Mera nam Lalith hai. — My name is Lalith.
Apka svagat hai. — You're welcome.

ARMENIAN

Barev. — Hello.
Inchpeses? — How are you?
Yes lavem. — I'm fine.
Ourakhem hantibel kez. — Pleased to meet you.
Anound inch e? — What's your name?
I'm anoune Alik e. — My name is Alik.
Bari akhorzhak. — Have a good meal.

HEBREW

Shalom. — Hello.
Ani beseder. — I'm fine.
Na'im me'od. — Pleased to meet you.
Eich koreim lecha? — What's your name?
Shmi Zev. — My name is Zev.
Behatslacha. — Good luck.

PASHTO

Khe chaare. — Hello.
Teh sengga yeh? — How are you?
Khe yem. — I'm fine.
Pe lee do moh khooshalaa
shwum. — Pleased to meet you.
Staa num tsa dhe? — What's your name?
Zama num Malala dhe. — My name is Malala.
Kha safer walare. — Have a good trip.

DARI

Salaam. — Hello.
Chi hal dared? — How are you?
Man khob astam. — I'm fine.
Khoshaal shodom az mulaqa
e shuma. — Pleased to meet you.
Esmetan chist? — What's your name?
Esmeman Jawid ast. — My name is Jawid.
Tashakor. — Thank you.

FARSI

Salam. — Hello.
Halet chetore? — How are you?
Man khubam. — I'm fine.
Khoshal shodam ke
mimbinamet. — Pleased to meet you.
Esmet cheyeh? — What's your name?
Esme man Nina. — My name is Nina.
Mamnoon. — Thank you.

TAJIK

Salom. — Hello.
Shumo chee khel? — How are you?
Naghz, ramat. — I'm fine.
Az vokhuriamon shod hastam. — Pleased to meet you.
Nomee shumo chist? — What's your name?
Nomee man Tarana. — My name is Tarana.
Khayr! — Goodbye!

RUSSIAN

Privét! — Hi!
Kak delá? — How are you?
Horosho! — I'm fine!
Ochen prijatno. — Pleased to meet you.
Kak teb'a zovut? — What's your name?
Men'a zovut Sasha. — My name is Sasha.
Prijatnovo appetita! — Enjoy your meal!

NEPALI

Namaste — Hello.
Tapaaii lai kasto cha? — How are you?
Malaai sanchai cha. — I'm fine.
Tapaaiilaaii bhetera
khushii laagyo. — Pleased to meet you.
Tapaaiiko naam ke ho? — What's your name?
Mero naam Abhichandra ho. — My name is Abhichandra.
Subha sandhya — Good evening.

NORTH AND CENTRAL AMERICA

ENGLISH (US)

Hello. — Hello.
How are you? — How are you?
I'm fine. — I'm fine.
Pleased to meet you. — Pleased to meet you.
What's your name? — What's your name?
My name is Kristy. — My name is Kristy.
Have a nice day! — Have a nice day!

FRENCH (CANADIAN)

Bonjour. — Hello.
Comment vas-tu? — How are you?
Bien! — I'm fine!
Enchantée! — Pleased to meet you!
Comment tu t'appelle? — What's your name?
Je m'appelle Elodie. — My name is Elodie.
Il fait froid. — It's cold.

DUTCH (C. AMERICAN)

Hallo. — Hello.
Hoe gaat het? — How are you?
Goed! — I'm fine!
Aangenaam kennis te maken. — Pleased to meet you.
Wat is jouw naam? — What's your name?
Mijn naam is Calvin. — My name is Calvin.
Tot ziens! — See you later!

SPANISH (MEXICO)

¡Hola! — Hello!
¿Cómo estás? — How are you?
Bien. — I'm fine.
Mucho gusto. — Pleased to meet you.
¿Cómo te llamas? — What's your name?
Me llamo Gabriel. — My name is Gabriel.
Adiós. — Goodbye.
Qué día tan soliado. — What a nice day.

ZAPOTEC

Xacza. — Hello.
Chíia xaquí. — Hi.
Xana nuu? — How are you?
Naa güenqui nuua. — I'm fine!
Rquitlaaszaa benbiaa Liuu. — Pleased to meet you.
Tu loo? — What's your name?
Naa láa Lluan. — My name is Lluan.
Xtiosteen. — Thank you.

OTOMI

Te gi jätho. — Hi.
¿Tengu gi ntini? — How are you?
Di 'bui xa hño. — I'm fine
Ndunthi di johya da pa'i — Pleased to meet you.
¿Te ri thuhu? — What's your name?
Ma thuhu Maria. — My name is Maria.
Jämadi. — Goodbye.

MAZAHUA

Kjimi. — Hello.
¿Jabi jyasü? — How are you?
Ri b'üntj'o najo'o. — I'm fine!
Najotj'o ri nzengwats'ü. — Pleased to meet you.
¿Pje ko ne chu'utsk'e? — What's your name?
In chu'uzgo Lupe. — My name is Lupe.
Pjokü. — Thank you.

CHINANTEC

E ju xá. — Hello.
¿A dxúnno? — How are you?
Jné dxúnna. — I'm fine.
Bíi dxé ki mali quínahné. — Pleased to meet you.
Hmíi xíinno? — What's your name?
Jné xíinna Péen. — My name is Péen.
Ma ánnu. — Thank you.

YUCATEC MAYA

Ba'ax ka wa'alik. — Hello.
Bix a beel? — How are you?
Tene' ma'alob aniken. — Tene' ma'alob aniken.
Ki'imak in wóol in
k'ajóotikech. — Pleased to meet you.
¿Bix a k'aaba'? — What's your name?
Tene' Carlos in k'aaba'. — My name is Carlos.
¡Ki'imak óolal tech! — Congratulations!

GARIFUNA

Buiti binafin. — Good morning.
Ida biangi? — How are you?
Magadietina. — I'm fine.
Gundana nasubu siunibu. — Pleased to meet you.
Ka biri? — What's your name?
Ara niri bai. — My name is Ara.
Buiti Bóustarun Irumu! — Happy Birthday!

MIXE

Sää. — Hello.
Sää mjatsï mkupetsï? — How are you?
Ka' sää. — I'm fine.
Ëyatp kuu napyäjtsïa'n. — Pleased to meet you.
Tii mxëëw? — What's your name?
Ana nxëëw. — My name is Ana.
Jats napyätkojmya'nt. — Well, see you later.

NGÄBERE

Ngantore. — Hello.
Monibiño? — How are you?
Tida kuin. — I'm fine.
Mokoinibi judotibodo. — Pleased to meet you.
Moko ño? — What's your name?
Tiko Mego. — My name is Mego.

TARAHUMARA

Kuiraba. — Hello.
Chu niri? — How are you?
Nejé Gará iyéna. — I'm fine.
We kaniri mi machisaa. — Pleased to meet you.
Chi mu rewéi? — What's your name?
Nejé rewéi Luiwisi. — My name is Luiwisi.
Mateterabá. — Thank you.

NAHUATL

Piali. — Hello.
Kenijkatsa tiitstok? — How are you?
Na kuali niitstok. — I'm fine.
Nipaki pampa nimitsixmati. — Pleased to meet you.
Kenijkatsa motoka? — What's your name?
Na notokaj Tonatiu. — My name is Tonatiu.
Tlaxkamati. — Thank you.
Timoitaseyok. — See you soon.

PUREPECHA

Nare chuskuki. — Hello.
Natsï jaraski? — How are you?
Ji sési jamaxaka. — I'm fine.
Tsípentasinka minarikunkeni. — Pleased to meet you.
Nare arhínasïni? — What's your name?
Ji arhínasïnkani Tsïtsïki. — My name is Tsïtsïki.

MISKITO

Naksa.	Hello.
Nakisma?	How are you?
Pain.	I'm fine.
Man ninam dia?	What's your name?
Yang ninam lika Jose.	My name is Jose.
Aisabe.	Goodbye.

HAWAIIAN

Aloha.	Hello.
Pehea 'oe?	How are you?
Maika'i nō.	I'm fine.
Hau'oli kēia hui 'ana o kāua.	Pleased to meet you.
'O wai kou inoa?	What's your name?
O Ailani ko'u inoa.	My name is Ailani.
Mālama pono.	Take care.

CREE

Ta'nisi.	Hello.
Ta'nisi?	How are you?
M'ona na'ntaw.	I'm fine.
Ki'htwa'm kawa'pamitin.	Pleased to meet you.
Kinana'skomitin.	Thank you.

MONTAGNAIS INNU

Kuei.	Hello.
Tan eshpanin?	How are you?
Niminupanin.	I'm fine.
Minuashiakanu.	Pleased to meet you.
Tan eshinikashuin?	What's your name?
Ishinikashu Mashku.	My name is Mashku.
Niaut.	Goodbye.

OJIBWE

Aniin.	Hello.
Aaniish naa ezhiyaayin?	How are you?
Nminoyaa gwa.	I'm fine.
Minogiizhigad.	Pleased to meet you.
Aaniin ezhinikaazoyan?	What's your name?
Leona Migwetch.	My name is Leona.
Giga-waabamin naaga.	See you later.

INUKTITUT

Ai.	Hello.
Qanuipit?	How are you?
Qaniungi.	I'm fine.
Alianaiq.	Pleased to meet you.
Kinauvit?	What's your name?
Quviagijara Paco.	My name is Paco.
Unukut.	Good evening.

YUP'IK

Waqaa.	Hello.
Cangacit?	How are you?
Assirtua.	I'm fine.
Mallrungin inglulgen.	Pleased to meet you.
Kiña ilviñ?	What's your name?
Wii-nga atqa Yaari.	My name is Yaari.
Quyana.	Thank you.

NAVAJO

Ya'at'eeh.	Hello.
Aa'?	How are you?
Ah nists'iid.	I'm fine.
Nizhonigo ałheehosiilzhid.	Pleased to meet you.
Haash yinilye?	What's your name?
Shi ei Nizhoni yinishye.	My name is Nizhoni.
Baa hozhoogo Nidizhchi!	Happy birthday!

SIOUX DAKOTA

Haw.	Hello.
Tangyang yaung hay?	How are you?
Wash tay.	I'm fine.
Wiyush kingyang wangchingyangkay.	Pleased to meet you.
Taku enichiyapi hay?	What's your name?
Sunktokeca emac'iyapi.	My name is Sunktokeca.
Doka!	See you later!

SIOUX LAKOTA

Haw.	Hello.
Tangyang yaung hay?	How are you?
Wash tay.	I'm fine.
Wiyush kingyang wangchingyangkay.	Pleased to meet you.
Taku enichiyapi hay?	What's your name?
Dyani emac'iyapi.	My name is Dyani.
Doka!	See you later!

ZUNI

Keshhi.	Hello.
Ko' do' dewanan deyaye?	How are you?
Ho' Meli leshhina.	My name is Meli.

CHEROKEE

Osiyo.	Hello.
Dohitsu?	How are you?
Osda.	I'm fine.
Gado detsa do a?	What's your name?
Adsila dagwa do.	My name is Adsila.
Donadagvhoi.	Goodbye.

HAITIAN CREOLE

Bonjou.	Good morning.
Kijan ou yé?	How are you?
Pa pi mal.	I'm fine.
Anchante.	Pleased to meet you.
Kijan ou rele?	What's your name?
Mwen rele Astryd.	My name is Astryd.
Bon apeti.	Enjoy your meal.

PAPIAMENTO

Halo.	Hello.
Con ta bai?	How are you?
Mi ta bon.	I'm fine.
Contento di mira bo.	Pleased to meet you.
Con yama bo?	What's your name?
Mi nomber ta Maudrith.	My name is Maudrith.
Bon nochi.	Good night.

CHOCTAW

Halito.	Hello.
Chim achukma?	How are you?
Achukma hoke.	I'm fine.
Chi hohchifo nanta?	What's your name?
Sa hohchifo ut Nitushi.	My name is Nitushi.
Yokoke.	Thank you.

SOUTH AMERICA

BRAZILIAN PORTUGUESE

Olá.	Hello
Como você está?	How are you?
Tudo bem.	I'm fine.
Muito prazer.	Pleased to meet you.
Qual é o seu nome?	What's your name?
Meu nome é João.	My name is João.
Até logo.	See you later.

FRENCH (S. AMERICAN)

Bonjour.	Hello.
Comment vas-tu?	How are you?
Bien!	I'm fine!
Enchantée!	Pleased to meet you!
Comment tu t'appelle?	What's your name?
Je m'appelle Elodie.	My name is Elodie.
Bon anniversaire!	Happy birthday!

DUTCH (S. AMERICAN)

Hallo.	Hello.
Hoe gaat het?	How are you?
Goed!	I'm fine!
Wat is jouw naam?	What's your name?
Mijn naam is Fleur.	My name is Fleur.
Fijne Verjaardag!	Happy birthday!
Tot ziens!	See you later!

ENGLISH (SURINAME)

Hello.	Hello.
How are you?	How are you?
I'm fine.	I'm fine.
Pleased to meet you.	Pleased to meet you.
What's your name?	What's your name?
My name is Ezra.	My name is Ezra.
Have a nice day!	Have a nice day!

WIZNAY

Amh'te na.	Hello.
Chiwo e'y?	How are you?
Ois thad.	I'm fine.
Wuj ta is t'a otafwed amej.	Pleased to meet you.
Chiwothe e'y?	What's your name?
Olhey thad.	My name is Olhey.
Isila Oisiyheja.	Thank you very much.

GUARANI

Maitei.	Hello.
Mba'éichapa reiko?	How are you?
Iporänte.	I'm fine.
Avy'aite roikuaávo.	Pleased to meet you.
Mba'éichapa nderéra?	What's your name?
Che réra Jasy.	My name is Jasy.
Aguyje.	Thank you.

YINE

Galu.	Hello.
Gipixkayi?	How are you?
Kigleno.	I'm fine.
Poyagnupotu numatyi.	Pleased to meet you.
Klo giwakyi?	What's your name?
Ngiwakni Rittma.	My name is Rittma.

QUECHUA

Napaykullayki.	Hello.
Imaynallan kashanki?	How are you?
Allillanmi.	I'm fine.
Anchatan kusikuni riqsispayki.	Pleased to meet you.
Iman sutiyki?	What's your name?
Izhi-n sutiy.	My name is Izhi.
Allin p'unchay kachun.	Have a good day.

MAPUDUNGUN

Mari mari pichi keche.	Hello.
Chumley eimi?	How are you?
Chumlen.	I'm fine.
Ayuwi tañi puike.	Pleased to meet you.
Iney pingeymi?	What's your name?
Iñche Elvira pingen.	My name is Elvira.
Chaltumay.	Thank you.

AYMARA

Kamisaki.	Hello.
Kunjamaskatasa?	How are you?
Hualiquithua.	I'm fine.
Ancha waliki.	Pleased to meet you.
Kunasa sutimaja?	What's your name?
Nayan sutijaj Severino.	My name is Severino.
Ccarurucama.	Thank you.

CARIB

Ujuu¡.	Hello.
¿Katukane ja?	How are you?
Ine Yakera wito.	I'm fine.
Ma riaba iji.	Pleased to meet you.
¿Bitu wai iji?	What's your name?
Ma wa Otoidanibo.	My name is Otoidanibo.

WAPISHANA
Tosh!	Hello!
Kaiman?	How are you?
Oo, kaiman.	I'm fine.
Na'apam pu'uu?	What's your name?
O'uu Masiki.	My name is Masiki.
Wicha kamoo.	The sun is hot.

EMBERA
Mena.	Hello.
Burá saúa?	How are you?
Bía búa.	I'm fine.
Mu.tʃo pla'θer.	Pleased to meet you.
Ke es tu 'nombre?	What's your name?
Mi 'nombre es Maria.	My name is Maria.
'gra.θjas.	Thank you.

SPANISH (S. AMER)
¡Hola!	Hello!
¿Cómo estás?	How are you?
Muy bien, gracias.	I'm fine.
¿Cómo te llamas?	What's your name?
Me llamo Gabriel.	My name is Gabriel.
Qué día tan hermoso!	What a beautiful day!

ARAWAK
Boili halakoba.	Hello.
Halika ba?	How are you?
Sakoa da.	I'm fine.
Neda-ko halekebñ babo.	Pleased to meet you.
Hamà b'iri?	What's your name?
Dai' iri Sabantho.	My name is Sabantho.

PAEZ
Ewcha.	Hello.
Ma'ucha?	How are you?

ASHANINKA
Nacabe.	Hello.
Tsika okantari pisaike?	How are you?
Nosaike kametsa.	I'm fine.
Kametsa ayotabaka.	Pleased to meet you.
Tsika pipaitaka?	What's your name?
Naka nopaita, Tsitsire.	My name is Tsitsire.

TICUNA
Numae.	Hello.
Ñuaküunta?	How are you?
Cha me.	I'm fine.
Kumaa cha taae kuuna cha dau.	Pleased to meet you.
Takui kuega?	What's your name?
Chauega nii.	My name is Chauega.
Moenchi.	Thanks

KUNA
Na.	Hello.
Be nuegambi?	How are you?
Eye, An nuegambi.	I'm fine.
Igui be nuga?	What's your name?
An Luisa nuga.	My name is Luisa.

GUAJIRO
Jamaya.	Hello.
Anayaasüje pia?	How are you?
Anasü taya	I'm fine.
Anasüja'a te'raajüin pia	Pleased to meet you
Kasaichit pünülia?	What's your name?
Tanulia Neimalu'u.	My name is Tanulia.

AFRICA

ARABIC
Marhabaan.	Hello.
Kayf halik?	How are you?
'Ana bikhayr.	I'm fine.
Ma ismik?	What's your name?
Inass ismee.	My name is Inass.
Shukraan.	Thank you.

SOMALI
Is ka warran.	Hello.
Sidee tahay?	How are you?
Waa nabad.	I'm fine.
Kulanti wanaagsan.	Pleased to meet you.
Magacca?	What's your name?
Magacaygu waa Amal.	My name is Amal.
Maalin wanaagsan.	Have a nice day.

BERBER
Azul.	Hello.
Amek id-tettiliḍ?	How are you?
Aqli-yi Labas.	I'm fine.
Farḥaɣ im-kwalaɣ/ im-kesnaɣ	Pleased to meet you.
Ism-ik?	What's your name?
Ism-iw Amaziɣ.	My name is AmaziÐ.
Tanmirt, qim-t d-lahna.	Thanks, see you.

AMHARIC
Salaam.	Hello.
Endamen allah?	How are you?
Dena nen.	I'm fine.
Selatawawaken das belonal.	Pleased to meet you.
Se-me man naw?	What's your name?
Se-me Meklit yibalal.	My name is Meklit.
Mälkam guzo.	Have a good trip.

OROMO
Akaam.	Hello.
Akam Jirtuu?	How are you?
Fayya.	I'm fine.
Si argun naaf gammachuda.	Pleased to meet you.
Maqaan ke eenyu?	What's your name?
Maqaan keeya Meti.	My name is Meti.
Galatoomi.	Thank you.

FULANI
Sannu.	Hello.
Jam na?	How are you?
Jam koo dume.	I'm fine.
Weli am andougo ma.	Pleased to meet you.
Noy inde ma?	What's your name?
Innde am Bari.	My name is Bari.
Sey yeso.	Goodbye.

IGBO
Ndewa.	Hello.
Kedu ka ímere?	How are you?
O di mma.	I'm fine.
Obu ihe obu uto imata gi.	Pleased to meet you.
Gini bu aha gi?	What's your name?
Aham bu Ebele.	My name is Ebele.
Anui ubosi omumu!	Happy birthday!

YORUBA
Pele o.	Hello.
She daadaa ni?	How are you?
Beeni.	I'm fine.
Inu mi dun lati pade re.	Pleased to meet you.
Ki ni oruko re?	What's your name?
Oruko mi ni Abeni.	My name is Abeni.
O da abo.	Goodbye.

AFRIKAANS
Hallo.	Hello.
Hoe gaan dit?	How are you?
Goed dankie.	I'm fine.
Bly te kenne.	Pleased to meet you.
Wat's jou naam?	What's your name?
My naam is Karel.	My name is Karel.
Totsiens.	See you later.

FRENCH (AFRICA)
Bonjour.	Hello.
Comment vas-tu?	How are you?
Bien!	I'm fine!
Enchantée!	Pleased to meet you!
Comment tu t'appelle?	What's your name?
Je m'appelle Pierre.	My name is Pierre.
Bon anniversaire!	Happy birthday!

HAUSA
Sannu.	Hello.
Kina lafiya?	How are you?
Lafiya lau.	I'm fine.
Na ji murnar saduwa da ke.	Pleased to meet you.
Ina sunnaka?	What's your name?
Sunana Azumi.	My name is Azumi.
Sai da safe.	Good night.

MALAGASY
Manao ahoana.	Hello.
Manao ahoana ianao?	How are you?
Tsara.	I'm fine.
Faly mahafantatra.	Pleased to meet you.
Iza no amaranao?	What's your name?
Felana na anarako.	My name is Felana.
Veloma.	Goodbye.

PORTUGUESE (AFRICA)
Ola!	Hi!
Como está?	How are you?
Bem!	I'm fine!
Prazer em conhecê-la.	Pleased to meet you.
Qual é seu nome?	What's your name?
O meu nome é Paula.	My name is Paula.
De onde você é?	Where are you from?

SWAHILI
Mambo.	Hello.
Habari yako?	How are you?
Nzuri.	I'm fine.
Nufurahi kukufahamu.	Pleased to meet you.
Jina lako nani?	What's your name?
Jina langu ni Jelani.	My name is Jelani.
Tutaonana.	Goodbye.

SHONA
Mhoroi.	Hello.
Makadii?	How are you?
Ndiripo.	I'm fine.
Ndafara kukuzivai.	Pleased to meet you.
Zita renyu ndiani?	What's your name?
Zita rangu ndinonzi Maita.	My name is Maita.
Ndingakutorei pikicha here?	Can I take a picture of you?

WOLOF
Salamou Alaykoum.	Hello.
Na nga def?	How are you?
Mangi fi rekk.	I'm fine.
Xamanté bi neexna ma.	Pleased to meet you.
Noo tudd?	What's your name?
Aminata laa tudd.	My name is Aminata.
Senegal laa jage.	I'm from Senegal.

ZULU

Sawubona.	Hello.
Unjani?	How are you?
Ngiyaphila.	I'm fine.
Ngiyajabula ukukwazi.	Pleased to meet you.
Ngubani igama lakho?	What's your name?
Igama lami ngingu-Langa.	My name is Langa.
Lo ngumfowethu.	This is my brother.

ENGLISH

English	English
Hello.	Hello.
How are you?	How are you?
I'm fine.	I'm fine.
Pleased to meet you.	Pleased to meet you.
What's your name?	What's your name?
My name is Bruce.	My name is Bruce.
Welcome to the party!	Welcome to the party!

CHICHEWA

Chichewa	English
Moni.	Hello.
Muli bwanji?	How are you?
Ndili bwino.	I'm fine.
Zicomo kukumana.	Pleased to meet you.
Dzina lako ndiwe ndani?	What's your name?
Dzina langa ndi Thoko.	My name is Thoko.
Tionana.	See you later.

TSWANA

Tswana	English
Dumela.	Hello.
Le kae?	How are you?
Re teng.	I'm fine.
Ke itumelela go goitsi.	Pleased to meet you.
O mang?	What's your name?
Leina la me ke Kgosi.	My name is Kgosi.
Boroko.	Good night.

OCEANIA

FIJIAN

Fijian	English
Bula!	Hello!
Vacava tiko?	How are you?
Bula Bula Vinaka Tiko.	I'm fine.
La ni bula.	Pleased to meet you!
O cei na yacamu?	What's your name?
Na yacaqu o Sereana.	My name is Sereano.
Da kana!	Enjoy your meal!

ARRERNTE

Arrernte	English
Werte.	Hello.
Unte mwerre?	How are you?
Ye, ayenge mwerre.	I'm fine.

FRENCH

French	English
Bonjour.	Hello.
Comment vas-tu?	How are you?
Bien!	I'm fine.
Enchantée!	Pleased to meet you!
Comment tu t'appelle?	What's your name?
Je m'appelle Michel.	My name is Michel.
Bon anniversaire!	Happy birthday!

TONGAN

Tongan	English
Mālō e lelei.	Hello.
Fēfē hake?	How are you?
Sai pē, mālō.	I'm fine.
Fiefia ke toe feiloaki mo koe.	Pleased to meet you.
Ko hai ho hingoa?	What's your name?
Ko hoku hingoa ko Maka.	My name is Maka.
Toki sio.	See you later!

HAWAIIAN

Hawaiian	English
Aloha.	Hello.
Pehea 'oe?	How are you?
Maika'i nō.	I'm fine.
Hau'oli kēia hui 'ana o kāua.	Pleased to meet you.
'O wai kou inoa?	What's your name?
'O Ailani ko'u inoa.	My name is Ailani.
Mālama pono.	Take care.

MAORI

Maori	English
Kiaora.	Hello.
Kei te pēhea koe?	How are you?
Kei te pai ahau.	I'm fine.
Pai ki te whakatau ia koe.	Pleased to meet you.
Ko wai tou ingoa?	What's your name?
Ko Ahora ahau.	My name is Ahora.
Kia pai tō ra.	Have a good day.

ENGLISH

English	English
Hello.	Hello.
How are you?	How are you?
I'm fine.	I'm fine.
Pleased to meet you.	Pleased to meet you.
What's your name?	What's your name?
My name is Rachel.	My name is Rachel.
Thank you.	Thank you.

AUSTRALIAN KRIOL

Australian Kriol	English
Hello.	Hello.
My name is Ali.	My name is Ali.

SAMOAN

Samoan	English
Tālofa.	Hello.
'O ā mai oe?	How are you?
'O Lelei au.	I'm fine.
Fiafia ua tā feiloa'i.	Pleased to meet you.
'O ai lou igoa?	What's your name?
'O lo'u igoa Talia.	My name is Talia.
Tōfā.	Goodbye.

TAHITIAN

Tahitian	English
'Iaorana.	Hello.
E aha tō 'oe huru?	How are you?
Maita'i	I'm fine.
Māuruuru I te fārereira'a.	Pleased to meet you.
'O vai tō 'oe i'oa?	What's your name?
'O Manuia tō'u i'oa.	My name is Manuia.

TAGALOG

Tagalog	English
Kumusta.	Hello.
Kumusta ka na?	How are you?
Mabuti naman ako.	I'm fine.
Ikinagagalak kong makilala ka.	Pleased to meet you.
Anong pangalan mo?	What's your name?
Ako si Shirley	My name is Shirley.
Magandang araw sa'yo!	Have a good day!

WARLPIRI

Warlpiri	English
Yuwa.	Hello.
Ngurrju - mayinpa?	How are you?
Yuwayi, ngurrjurna.	I'm fine.
Ngakarnangku nyanyi.	See you later.

TOK PISIN

Tok Pisin	English
Halo.	Hello.
Yu stap gut?	How are you?
Mi stap gut.	I'm fine.
Gutpela long bungim yu.	Pleased to meet you.
Husat nem bilong yu?	What's your name?
Nem bilong ni emi Mekere.	My name is Mekere.
Tenkyu.	Thank you.

TIWI

Tiwi	English
Awungana!	Hello!
Awungana nginja?	How are you?
Ngija papuka.	I'm fine.
Nimpangi.	Goodbye.

YOLNGU

Yolngu	English
Hey.	Hello.
Nhamirri nhe?	How are you?
Djulngi ga.	I'm fine.
Makarr yun gumurr yun nhe.	Pleased to meet you.
Nha nhenbal garrar?	What's your name?
Bubu.	Goodbye.

ANTARCTICA

ENGLISH (ANTARCTICA)

English	English
Hello.	Hello.
How are you?	How are you?
I'm fine.	I'm fine.
Pleased to meet you.	Pleased to meet you.
What's your name?	What's your name?
My name is Zack.	My name is Zack.
I'm cold!	I'm cold!

FRENCH (ANTARCTICA)

French	English
Bonjour.	Hello.
Comment vas-tu?	How are you?
Bien!	I'm fine!
Enchantée!	Pleased to meet you!
Comment tu t'appelle?	What's your name?
Je m'appelle Marie.	My name is Marie.
Bon anniversaire!	Happy birthday!

SWEDISH (ANTARCTICA)

Swedish	English
Hej!	Hello!
Hur är det?	How are you?
Bra!	I'm fine!
Trevligt att träffas.	Pleased to meet you.
Vad heter du?	What's your name?
Jag heter Elin.	My name is Elin.
Varifrån kommer du?	Where do you come from?

GERMAN (ANTARCTICA)

German	English
Guten Tag.	Hello.
Wie gehts?	How are you?
Gut!	I'm fine!
Schön, dich kennen zu lernen.	Pleased to meet you.
Wie heißt du?	What's your name?
Ich heiße Ava.	My name is Ava.
Schüß.	Goodbye.

RUSSIAN (ANTARCTICA)

Russian	English
Privét!	Hello!
Kak delá?	How are you?
Horosho!	I'm fine!
Ochen prijatno.	Pleased to meet you.
Kak teb'a zovut?	What's your name?
Men'a zovut Leon.	My name is Leon.
Prijatnovo appetita!	Bon appetit!

NORWEGIAN (ANTARCTICA)

Norwegian	English
Hei!	Hello!
Hvordan har du det?	How are you?
Takk, bare bra.	I'm fine.
Hyggelig å treffe deg.	Pleased to meet you.
Hva heter du?	What's your name?
Jeg heter Karin.	My name is Karin.

SPANISH (ANTARCTICA)

Spanish	English
¡Hola!	Hello!
¿Cómo estás?	How are you?
Bien!	I'm fine!
Encantada.	Pleased to meet you.
¿Cómo te llamas?	What's your name?
Me llamo Raquel.	My name is Raquel.
Fuera hace mucho frío.	It's cold outside.

First published in the U.S.A. in 2016 by
Wide Eyed Editions, an imprint of Quarto Inc.,
276 Fifth Avenue, Suite 206, New York, NY 10001
QuartoKnows.com
Visit our blogs at QuartoKnows.com

ISBN 978-1-84780-863-9

The artworks were drawn digitally
Set in Helvetica Neue, Triplex and Mr Cyrk

Designed by Nicola Price
Edited by Jenny Broom
Published by Rachel Williams

Printed in Dongguan, Guangdon, China

1 3 5 7 9 8 6 4 2